US SPECIAL FORCES

PARARESCUEMEN

By Mark A. Harasymiw

Gareth Stevens
Publishing

Please visit our website, www.garethstevens.com. For a free color catalog of all our high-quality books, call toll free 1-800-542-2595 or fax 1-877-542-2596.

Library of Congress Cataloging-in-Publication Data

Harasymiw, Mark.
Pararescuemen / Mark A. Harasymiw.
     p. cm. — (US Special Forces)
Includes index.
ISBN 978-1-4339-6571-5 (pbk.)
ISBN 978-1-4339-6572-2 (6-pack)
ISBN 978-1-4339-6569-2 (library binding)
1. United States. Air Force—Search and rescue operations—Juvenile literature. 2. Parachute troops—Juvenile literature. 3. Search and rescue operations—Juvenile literature. 4. Special forces (Military science)—United States—Juvenile literature. I. Title.
UG633.H359 2012
358.4'1343—dc23

                                    2011037102

First Edition

Published in 2012 by
Gareth Stevens Publishing
111 East 14th Street, Suite 349
New York, NY 10003

Designer: Michael J. Flynn
Editor: Kristen Rajczak

Photo credits: Courtesy of US Air Force: Cover, pp. 1 by Master Sgt. Daniel Farrell, 4–5 by Master Sgt. Kevin J. Gruenwald, 5, 7 by Staff Sgt. Ricky A. Bloom, 8–9, 11 by Staff Sgt. Steve McGill, 13 by Staff Sgt. Lakisha A. Croley, 15 by Airman 1st Class Veronica Pierce, 16–17 by Staff Sgt. Nathan Allen, 17, 18 by Staff Sgt. Desiree N. Palacios, 19 by Staff Sgt. Matthew Rosine, 20 by Staff Sgt. Jacob N. Bailey, 21 by Tech. Sgt. Ruby Zarzyczny, 22 by Master Sgt. Lance S. Cheung, 23 by Staff Sgt. Clay Lancaster, 25 by Master Sgt. Val Gempis, 27, 28–29 by Staff Sgt. Christopher Boitz; p. 10 Alfred Batungbacal/ Time & Life Pictures/Getty Images; p. 24 Shutterstock.com.

Printed in the United States of America

CPSIA compliance information: Batch #CW12GS: For further information contact Gareth Stevens, New York, New York at 1-800-542-2595.

CONTENTS

Words in the glossary appear in **bold** type the first time they are used in the text.

THE AIR FORCE

The US Air Force is the newest branch of the US military. It started as part of the army. In 1947, the United States recognized that airpower had become a major factor in modern conflicts and the air force needed to be an independent branch of the military.

The air force's **mission** is to fly and fight in air, space, and **cyberspace**. It uses highly trained pilots to fly planes to protect and support US ground forces. The air force has many units of airmen working toward this mission. One of these units is made up of brave airmen called pararescuemen.

Skilled Airmen

Pararescuemen, or PJs (short for parajumpers), are some of the most skilled airmen in the world. While other US Special Forces units—such as Navy SEALs, Army Rangers, and Green Berets—are trained to attack the enemy, the PJs' first job is to help downed airmen and other injured soldiers.

The *para* in the word "pararescuemen" comes from what these airmen do best—parachuting!

5

THE BRAVE PJS

US Air Force Pararescuemen don't just perform rescue operations. They're **emergency** medical **technicians** (EMTs) and paramedics with a mission to search for and treat injured soldiers. They're trained to work in all kinds of conditions and handle many kinds of injuries—all while risking their lives.

PJs travel to their patients by airplane, helicopter, or parachute. They may even use diving gear if they have to rescue someone in the water! Sometimes their missions include avoiding or even fighting enemy soldiers, especially if it means protecting their patients.

AFSOC

The Air Force Special Operations Command (AFSOC) is the branch of the air force responsible for overseeing PJs as well as other Air Force Special Forces. AFSOC troops are part of many missions, from helping air forces in other countries to taking supplies and fuel to US troops.

Pararescuemen ready other airmen for transport during a training exercise in Africa.

FIRST PJ MISSION

The first US pararescue mission occurred in 1943 during the height of World War II. A group of airmen needed to be rescued after they parachuted out of their plane before it crashed near the border between China and Burma.

Pararescue in the Jungle

Lieutenant Colonel Flickinger and the medics with him faced many problems besides locating the airmen and treating their injuries. In the area of jungle where the men crashed were enemy soldiers and bloodsucking animals such as leeches, mosquitoes, and ticks. There were some local people who were friendly, however, and they helped the US airmen.

The downed airmen were in a jungle far away from any roads or trails. The only way to reach them was by parachute. Lieutenant Colonel Don Flickinger and two medical specialists parachuted into the jungle to locate the airmen and treat their injuries. More than a month later, the group was led out of the jungle to safety.

Early parajumpers leap from a plane during the 1940s.

9

IN THE WAR ZONE

Pararescuemen also aided the US military in other conflicts. They served bravely in both the **Korean War** and the **Vietnam War**.

Airmen load injured soldiers into a helicopter during the Vietnam War.

During the Vietnam War, PJs used helicopters to complete their missions. Much of the Vietnam War was fought in the jungle. Helicopters were able to **hover** over injured soldiers so pararescuemen could safely drop to them. PJs used cables to lower themselves to the ground to take care of soldiers' injuries. Then PJs and injured soldiers were pulled up to the helicopter. This was dangerous because enemy soldiers often shot at helicopters while they were hovering.

The Gulf War

In the early 1990s, pararescuemen saved airmen during the Gulf War. US Air Force troops were a big part of this operation against Iraq. They bombed the enemy and carried supplies. The PJs used helicopters again during their missions to find and treat downed pilots and wounded airmen.

Pararescuemen also rescue people who are in trouble outside of war zones. Pararescue teams helped many people after a 1989 earthquake in San Francisco, California, and after Hurricane Katrina hit the Gulf Coast in 2005. After a terrible earthquake in Haiti in 2010, pararescuemen and similar teams from many other countries helped bring aid to people who needed it.

Gemini 8

PJs have even helped rescue astronauts! In 1966, the Gemini 8 mission team was forced to land their spacecraft in the Pacific Ocean. Pararescuemen used special **equipment** to help the spacecraft stay afloat until a navy ship could arrive to pick up the astronauts and the pararescuemen.

PJs rescue people who have accidents in hard-to-reach areas, too. In 2011, a pararescue team from Kirtland Air Force Base searched a mountainous area of Colorado for a missing hiker. She had been lost for 2 days when pararescuemen used a helicopter to rescue her.

PJs are trained to perform medical treatments and rescue missions in mountains, jungles, deserts, oceans, cities, and the Arctic.

PJ QUALIFICATIONS

Airmen who want to become pararescuemen must pass a tough physical test to be able to start PJ training. This test is called the Physical Abilities and Stamina Test (PAST). As part of that test, an airman must complete the following in 3 hours or less:

- Swim 27.3 yards (25 m) underwater on one breath
- Swim 1,093.6 yards (1,000 m) sidestroke or freestyle in 26 minutes or less
- Run 1.5 miles (2.4 km) in under 10 minutes and 30 seconds
- 8 chin-ups in a minute or less
- 50 sit-ups in 2 minutes or less
- 50 flutter kicks in 2 minutes or less

Other Requirements

Not only must a PJ candidate be in top physical shape to begin training, but he must also meet other requirements. First, only men can become PJs. Second, PJ candidates must be high school graduates. They must be able to see really well, too. Finally, PJs must be US citizens.

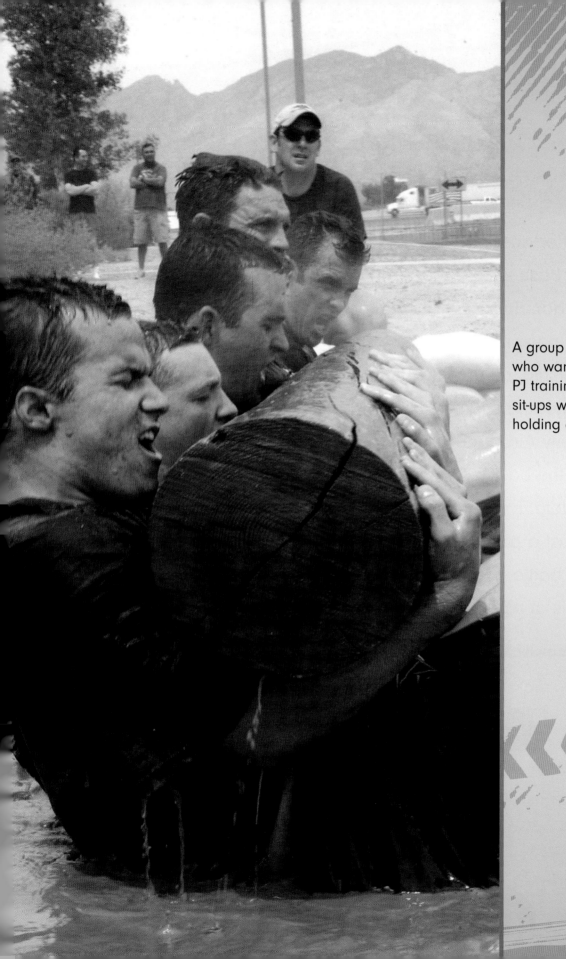

A group of men who want to enter PJ training perform sit-ups while holding a log.

TRAINING

After passing the PAST, PJ trainees report to Lackland Air Force Base in Texas for the Pararescue Preparatory Course and the **Indoctrination** Course. For 3 months, they train hard and learn many skills, such as using medical terms and exercising leadership, all of which help them in later training.

After the courses at Lackland, PJ candidates attend the US Army Airborne School at Fort Benning, Georgia. There, they learn the basics of parachuting. To pass, each soldier must complete five parachute jumps. Two jumps are during the day with just a parachute and **reserve parachute**. Three jumps are in full battle gear. Two of these are during the day. The final jump is at night.

PJs parachute over Fort Benning in 2010.

The Maroon Beret

Airmen require months of training in order to earn the right to be called pararescuemen. After completing the training, they earn the honor of wearing a special maroon hat called a beret. They're the only group in the US military that's allowed to wear a beret of that color.

These airmen are wearing the dive gear PJs learn to use during combat diver school.

After learning basic parachuting skills, PJ trainees travel to US Air Force Combat Diver School in Panama City, Florida. There, they spend 6 weeks learning how to use different kinds of diving equipment. They also learn how to use that equipment to sneak into areas controlled by the enemy and search for downed airmen. They practice these skills in water up to 130 feet (40 m) deep!

After this, they attend the US Navy Underwater Egress Training where they learn how to escape from an aircraft that has crashed into the water.

In the Wild

Training isn't over yet! PJ trainees next head west to US Air Force Basic Survival School at Fairchild Air Force Base in Washington State, where they learn to live in the wilderness. This 19-day-long course teaches PJs how to work in any **environment** and make their way back to friendly forces.

These airmen built a raft to keep their packs dry during an air force survival competition.

19

PJs must train for many different kinds of missions because parachute jumps often occur during dangerous situations.

After survival school in Washington, trainees go to Freefall Parachutist School at Fort Bragg, North Carolina. At Fort Bragg, the PJ trainees learn special parachuting skills, such as air **maneuvers** and how to handle free fall, or the part of the parachute drop before the parachute opens.

PJ candidates then go to the Yuma Proving Grounds in Arizona where they learn more advanced parachutist skills. They practice both day and night drops as well as jumping at high and low **altitudes**. When performing the highest of the jumps, the PJs have to carry oxygen tanks with them so they can breathe!

Medical Training

After advanced parachute training, the PJ trainees go to the Paramedic Course for 22 weeks. Here they learn how to provide emergency medical treatment. Next, the PJs attend the Pararescue Recovery Specialist Course in New Mexico for 24 weeks. They learn to give medical care in the field and practice rescues using a helicopter.

PJs like these continue to practice rescue and survival skills throughout their military careers.

HALO PARACHUTING

One of the advanced parachuting skills PJs learn at Yuma is called HALO parachuting. "HALO" stands for high-altitude, low-opening.

When a PJ makes a HALO jump, he leaps from an aircraft that's 35,000 feet (10.67 km) in the air and doesn't open his parachute until he's only 2,500 feet (762 m) above the ground. This makes it harder for an enemy to detect a PJ because he's traveling very fast for most of his drop. Besides bringing oxygen along on his drop, the PJ has a special machine on his parachute that opens it when he reaches the right altitude.

A PJ readies himself for a HALO jump.

HAHO Parachuting

"HAHO" stands for high-altitude, high-opening. PJs jump from aircraft flying up to 35,000 feet (10.67 km) and open their parachutes after only a few seconds of free fall. Since they open their parachutes so high, the PJs float down quietly. They're often able to drift behind enemy lines undetected.

GETTING AROUND

PJs use different kinds of **vehicles** in their missions. Rescue helicopters were first used in World War II. These first helicopters carried injured soldiers on stretchers to safety. As helicopter technology improved, PJs had access to faster helicopters that could carry more passengers for greater distances.

However, the air force plans to replace many helicopters, including the PJs' helicopters, with the CV-22 Osprey. The Osprey is called a tilt-rotor aircraft. This means that the pilot can change the position of the rotors, which are the parts that make the aircraft fly. This allows it to take off without a runway like a helicopter, but fly long distances like an airplane.

CV-22 Osprey

Gear

PJs carry a lot of gear on their missions, sometimes even including diving equipment! A PJ's pack is full of medical supplies used to treat their patients. They also need night-vision goggles to help them see in the dark on night missions. And, in case they meet enemy soldiers, PJs also carry guns.

PJ HEROES

PJs are the toughest and most skilled medics in the US military. Many have done their job bravely in very dangerous conditions.

Bill Pitsenbarger was a 21-year-old pararescueman who served during the Vietnam War. In April 1966, enemy soldiers surrounded a group of US soldiers. Pitsenbarger and his unit flew to the battle in a helicopter, ready to rescue wounded soldiers. With the air thick with bullets, Pitsenbarger volunteered to help the injured soldiers into the helicopter. He then stayed behind to aid soldiers on the ground. The helicopter later returned for him, but he had been killed.

Air Force Cross

The Air Force Cross is awarded to a US Air Force airmen for extraordinary heroism. In 1966, Bill Pitsenbarger received the Air Force Cross for saving the lives of several soldiers. In 2000, this honor was upgraded to the highest award in the US military—the Medal of Honor.

Bill Pitsenbarger was part of more than 250 missions during the Vietnam War.

PARARESCUEMEN MOTTO

The motto of the pararescuemen is "That Others May Live." This motto describes the PJs' commitment to saving other peoples' lives even in dangerous situations. They have risked their lives saving fellow US soldiers and citizens of other nations since World War II.

A group of pararescuemen train for a mission in Afghanistan in 2010.

Today, US Air Force Pararescuemen continue to support US military actions all over the world. They give medical aid to those who need it and perform rescue missions for soldiers and US citizens alike. If it weren't for these brave members of the Special Forces, many people would have lost their lives.

The Flash

On each PJ's maroon beret is a flash, or small patch sometimes made of metal, displaying the pararescue motto, "That Others May Live." It shows a picture of a parachute above a guardian angel wrapping its arms around the world.

GLOSSARY

altitude: height above sea level

cyberspace: the online world of computer networks; the Internet

emergency: an unexpected situation that needs quick action

environment: surroundings

equipment: tools, clothing, and other items needed for a job

hover: to float in the air without moving around much

indoctrination: the act of teaching the ideas or beliefs of a group

Korean War: a conflict between North and South Korea that began in 1950 and ended in 1953

maneuver: a planned movement of a military unit

mission: a task or job a group must perform

reserve parachute: an extra parachute carried in case the main parachute doesn't work properly

technician: a person skilled at a job

vehicle: an object used for carrying or transporting people or goods, such as a car, truck, or airplane

Vietnam War: a conflict starting in 1955 and ending in 1975 between South Vietnam and North Vietnam in which the United States joined with South Vietnam

FOR MORE INFORMATION

Books

Montana, Jack. *Parachute Regiment*. Broomall, PA: Mason Crest Publishers, 2011.

Sandler, Michael. *Pararescuemen in Action*. New York, NY: Bearport Publishing, 2008.

Sutherland, Adam. *Special Forces*. Minneapolis, MN: Lerner Publications, 2012.

Websites

How the U.S. Air Force Works
www.howstuffworks.com/air-force.htm
Read about the air force and its missions around the world.

USAF Pararescue
www.pararescue.com
This website provides information about PJs, both current and historical.

Publisher's note to educators and parents: Our editors have carefully reviewed these websites to ensure that they are suitable for students. Many websites change frequently, however, and we cannot guarantee that a site's future contents will continue to meet our high standards of quality and educational value. Be advised that students should be closely supervised whenever they access the Internet.

INDEX